# Rosa Parks

## TAKES A STAND

McGraw Hill SRA

*Columbus, OH*

**Cover** © PAUL SANCYA/AFP/Getty Images; **3** © Stephen Saks
Photography / Alamy; **4, 5** © Bettmann/CORBIS; **6** © Hank Walker/
Time Life Pictures/Getty Images; **7** © AP Photo/Gene Herrick; **8** ©
Grey Villet/Time & Life Pictures/Getty Images; **9** © Photo by Don
Cravens/Time Life Pictures/Getty Images; **10** © David Ball / Alamy;
**11** © PAUL SANCYA/AFP/Getty Images.

**SRAonline.com**

 **SRA**

Printed in China.

Send all inquiries to this address:
SRA/McGraw-Hill
4400 Easton Commons
Columbus, OH 43219

ISBN: 978-0-07-608570-5
MHID: 0-07-608570-8

1 2 3 4 5 6 7 8 9 NOR 13 12 11 10 09 08 07

*The McGraw-Hill Companies*

One day in 1955 Rosa Parks made history. She wouldn't give up her seat on a bus.

At that time laws in the South were not fair. They kept blacks and whites apart. Black citizens were not treated as well as white citizens.

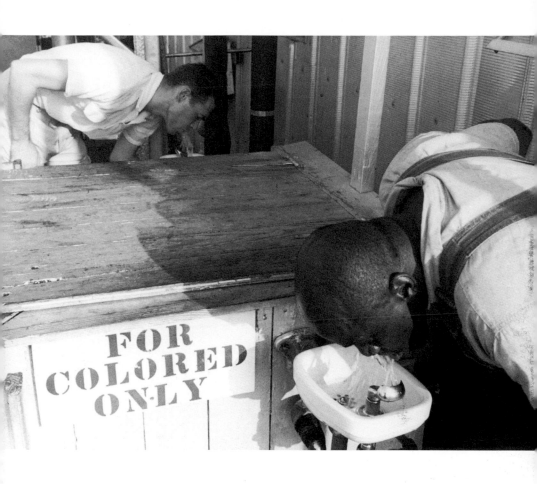

Blacks couldn't go to white schools. They couldn't eat in the same parts of restaurants. They had to use different water fountains.

Black people had to sit in the back seats on buses. They had to stand up if a white person needed a seat.

The bus driver told Parks to stand. She said no. Parks was arrested for breaking a rule she felt was wrong.

Other African Americans heard about Parks.
They would stop using, or boycott, the buses.

Black people walked to work. They rode with friends or on horses. But they would not take a bus. This went on for a year!

Parks's case went to the Supreme Court. The court ruled. Parks won! Laws that kept people apart were wrong.

Rosa Parks helped start the fight for equal rights. She showed what one person can do.

# Vocabulary

**laws** (lôz) (page 4) *n.* Plural form of **law:** A rule made by a government.

**fair** (fâr) (page 4) *adj.* Not favoring one more than another.

**citizens** (sit´ i zenz) (page 4) *n.* Plural form of **citizen:** A person who was born in a country or who chooses to live in and become a member of a country.

**treated** (trēt´ əd) (page 4) *v.* Past tense of **treat:** To behave toward or deal with in a certain way.

**arrested** (ə res´ təd) (page 7) *v.* Past tense of **arrest:** To hold by authority of the law.

**boycott** (boi´ kot) (page 8) *v.* To refuse to buy or do something until certain conditions are improved.

## Comprehension Focus:
## Making Inferences

**1.** How do you think Rosa Parks felt that day on the bus?

**2.** How do you think the bus boycott affected the rest of the country?